WRIT
ABOUT MATH

Activities Based on the
Common Core Standards

Written by Rebecca Stark
Illustrated by Karen Birchak

The purchase of this book entitles the individual teacher to reproduce copies of the student pages for use in his or her classroom exclusively. The reproduction of any part of the work for an entire school or school system or for commercial use is prohibited.

ISBN 978-1-56644-449-1

TABLE OF CONTENTS

Standards

MATHEMATICS CORE STANDARDS: ACTIVITIES 1–100
(Numbers refer to activity Numbers, not page numbers.)

Apply and extend understandings of multiplication and division to multiply and divide fractions.   26, 29, 30, 34, 89, 90, 92

Apply the area and perimeter formulas for rectangles in real world mathematical problems.   45, 59, 98

Classify shapes by properties of their lines and angles.   4, 13, 42, 43

Convert among different-sized standard measurement units within a given measurement system and use these conversions in solving multi-step, real-world problems.   18, 19, 45, 60, 64, 65, 78, 87

Determine whether a given whole number in the range of 1–100 is prime or composite.   76

Draw and identify lines and angles.   24, 37, 39, 46, 95

Explain patterns in the number of zeros of the product when multiplying a number by powers of 10.   6, 7, 12

Explain patterns in the placement of the decimal point when a decimal is multiplied or divided by a power of 10.   7

Extend understanding of fraction equivalence.   10, 25, 52, 66, 83, 99

Find a percent of a quantity as a rate of 100.   23, 34, 40, 41, 74, 80, 88, 93, 94

Find the area of special quadrilaterals by composing into rectangles or decomposing into triangles and other shapes.   38, 43

Find the volume of a right rectangular prism.   91

Fluently add and subtract multi-digit whole numbers.   22

Fluently divide multi-digit numbers.   48, 79

Gain familiarity with factors and multiples.   31, 54, 76

Generate and analyze patterns.   27, 47

Interpret multiplication as scaling (resizing) by explaining why multiplying a given number by a fraction less than 1 results in a product smaller than the given number.   53

Know the formulas for the area and circumference of a circle and use them to solve problems.   44, 58, 7

5Measure angles in whole-number degrees using a protractor.   35

Perform arithmetic operations in the conventional order when there are no parentheses to specify a particular order.   49

Read, write and compare decimals to thousands.   8, 40, 50, 52, 55

Recognize that in a multi-digit number, a digit in one place represents 10 times as much as it represents in the place to its right and 1/10 of what it represents in the place to its left.   82

Recognize a line of symmetry for a two-dimensional figure.   17

Represent and interpret data.   5, 9, 69, 72, 77, 81

Solve mathematical problems involving area, surface area and volume.   1, 2, 15, 21, 38, 73, 91, 98

Solve multistep word problems posed with whole numbers and having whole-number answers using the four operations.   56

Solve problems involving addition and subtraction of fractions referring to the same whole and having like denominators.   85,

Solve problems involving finding the whole, given a part and the percent.   28, 61

Solve real world problems involving division of unit fractions by non-zero numbers and division of whole numbers by unit fractions.   62, 68

Solve word problems involving addition and subtraction of fractions referring to the same whole, including cases of unlike denominators (including mixed numbers).   67, 70, 78, 87, 99

Solve word problems involving division of numbers leading to answers in the form of fractions or mixed numbers.   96

Solve word problems involving money.   23, 51, 88

Summarize and describe distributions.   11, 14, 19, 31, 41, 57

Understand concepts of angle and measure angles.   35, 36, 46

Understand concepts of volume and relate volume to multiplication and division.   91

Understand the concept of ratio and use ratio language to describe a ratio relationship between two quantities.   12, 40, 38, 83

Understand the place value system.   6, 7, 8, 12, 63

Understand the relationship between addition and subtraction.   20, 22

Use the four operations to solve word problems involving intervals of time.   3, 19, 84

Although not so marked, activities also address the standards of good mathematical practices:

- Make sense of problems and persevere in solving them.
- Reason abstractly and quantitatively.
- Construct viable arguments and critique the reasoning of others.
- Model with mathematics.
- Use appropriate tools strategically.
- Attend to precision.
- Look for and make use of structure.
- Look for and express regularity in repeated reasoning.

CRITICAL AND CREATIVE THINKING: ACTIVITIES 100–120

The critical-and-creative thinking activities as well as many of the math activities also address some or all of these language arts core standards:

- Write informative/explanatory texts to examine a topic and convey ideas and information clearly.
- Provide reasons that are supported by facts and details.
- Use precise language and domain-specific vocabulary to inform about or explain the topic.

WEEDS IN THE GARDEN

1. You have planted a garden and notice that a rectangular area of the garden is covered with weeds. In order to determine how much weed killer to buy, you must figure out how many square yards are in your garden. Explain how you will determine the number of square yards.

A HOME FOR MY FISH

2. You want to buy a larger aquarium for your fish. You know that the one you have has a volume of 4,608 cubic inches. The one you are looking at measures 20" x 12" x 12". You want to know if it has a greater volume than the one you have at home. How will you find out?

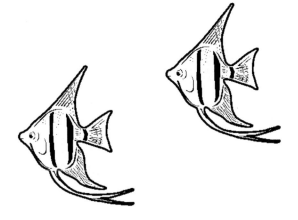

A CLOSE CALL!

3. You wake up at 7 a.m. The school bus will leave your stop at 8:15 sharp. It takes you 70 minutes to get ready and get to the bus stop. Will you be at the bus stop in time to make the bus? Explain how you know.

SYLLOGISMS

4. Complete this syllogism:

    A. All rectangles have four right interior angles.

    B. Squares are a sub-category of rectangles.

    C. Therefore, _____.

Then write an original syllogism using other shapes.

FAVORITE SPORTS

5. The chart below shows the percentage of sixth graders in Valley Middle School who favor each sport. In complete sentences, write everything you can learn from studying the chart.

Favorite Sports of 240 Sixth-grade Students of Valley Middle School

© Educational Impressions, Inc.

MULTIPLY BY TEN
6. What is the easiest way to solve these problems? Explain why.

$$10 \times 2{,}560 =$$
$$100 \times 2{,}560 =$$
$$1{,}000 \times 2{,}560 =$$

DIVIDE BY TEN
7. What is the easiest way to solve this problem? Explain what we are really doing when we divide 2,560 by 10.

$$2{,}560 \div 10 =$$

WHAT DOES IT REALLY MEAN?

9. Use < or > to compare these numbers. Write out the largest number in expanded form. In other words, explain exactly what each digit means. For example, 238 means there are 2 hundreds, 3 tens and 8 ones.

86.582   8,658.2   865.82

FAVORITE ZOO ANIMALS

9. Take a survey to find out your classmates' favorite zoo animals. Then write a summary of your findings.

SO MANY TEETH

10. The normal adult mouth has 8 incisors, 4 canines, 8 premolars, 8 molars and 4 wisdom teeth. Suppose a person who has all of his teeth has all 4 wisdom teeth removed. What fraction of the original number of teeth remain? How would you figure this out?

KOALAS

11. Koalas are found in the wild in eastern Australia. Those in the cooler southern areas are bigger and have thicker fur than those of the north. Southern koalas weigh between 9 and 14 kilograms, and northern ones weigh between 6 and 7 kilograms. Suppose you wanted to know the range of weight of all koalas in pounds. How would you figure it out?

CAMPAIGN SPENDING

12. You read in the newspaper that the ratio of campaign spending of Candidate A to Candidate B is 10 to 1. Suppose Candidate B spent $100,000. Explain how you would find out how much Candidate A spent.

Candidate A: $?
Candidate B: $100,000

SO MANY TRIANGLES

13. List as many different kinds of triangles as you can. Compare and contrast them.

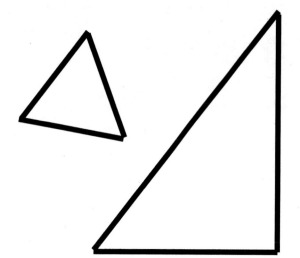
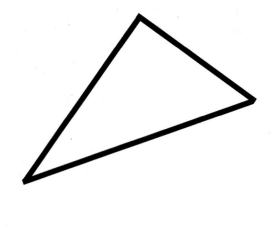

HOW DOES MY SCORE COMPARE?

14. Emma got a 93 on her math test. She wants to know how her grade compares to those of her classmates. Below is a list of all the students' test scores. How will Emma determine the mode, median, mean and range of the scores?

89	86	100
67	78	98
70	93	99
94	91	67
82	86	90
65	75	89
90	82	92
89	88	70

WILL THEY FIT?

15. Josh has been given a bag of blocks. It says on the bag that there are 500 blocks and that each block is 1 cubic centimeter. He would like to store them in a box that is 8 centimeters high, 8 centimeters wide, and 8 centimeters deep. Explain how Josh can determine whether or not the box will hold all of the blocks.

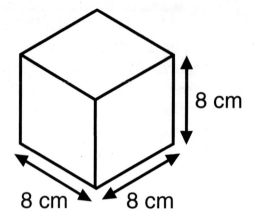

8 cm

8 cm   8 cm

CHANGE OF A DOLLAR

16. How many different ways can you think of to make change for a dollar without using more than 5 pennies? Write complete sentences.

SYMMETRY

17. Explain what is meant by symmetry. Use the figures below to help you write your explanation.

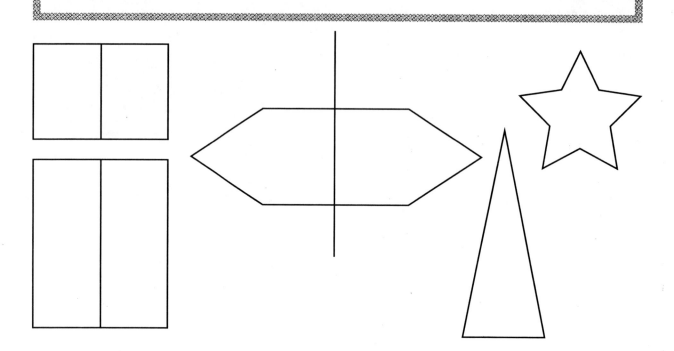

WHO'S TALLER?

18. You and your friends decide to measure each other to see who is the tallest. Jessie is excited because at 5'3" she thinks she is the tallest. Rebecca says that Jessie is not the tallest. She says that at 64" in height, she is the tallest. As another of the friends, explain to Jessie or Rebecca why she is wrong.

A WALK IN SPACE

19. As of June 11, 2011, NASA astronaut Michael "Mike" Fincke had logged 1,189 minutes of EVA (Extravehicular Activity) time on nine spacewalks. How would you figure out how much time in hours and minutes he spent on those spacewalks? How would you figure out the average amount of time spent on each walk?

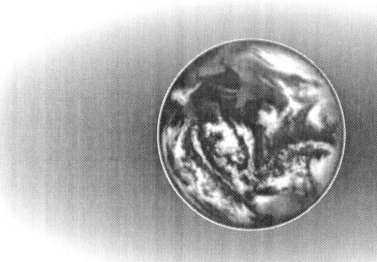

ANALOGIES

20. Compare and contrast addition and subtraction. Then create some analogies using the terms *addition* and *subtraction* either on the same side of the "::" or on opposite sides.

Addition : _____ :: Subtraction : _____

Addition : Subtraction :: _____ : _____

MORE ANALOGIES

21. Compare and contrast multiplication and division. Then create some analogies using the terms *multiplication* and *division* either on the same side of the "::" or on opposite sides.

Multiplication : _____ :: Division : _____

Multiplication : Division :: _____ : _____

A LESSON IN SUBTRACTION

22. Sophie's brother is having trouble with this subtraction problem and her mother has asked her to help him. What step-by-step directions will she give him to help him solve the problem? What explanation will she give him to teach him how to check his answer?

$$\begin{array}{r} 1358 \\ -789 \\ \hline \end{array}$$

ON SALE

23. You see that your favorite video store is having a sale. Everything is 50% off! You have $75 to spend and want to buy three games. The regular price for two of the games is $60 each. The regular price of the third game is $40. You do not think you have enough money. Your friend says that he will lend you the money so that you can buy the games. How will you figure out how much money you will have to borrow from your friend?

All Video Games
ON SALE
50% Off!

24. Create a a matching game using the angles below. Be sure to include instructions.

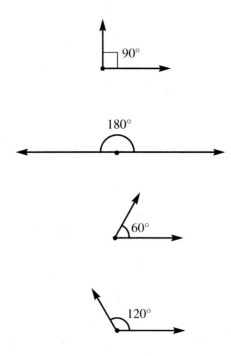

1/4 OR 9/36?

25. Jan brings 36 doughnuts to school for her birthday. When everyone has finished eating, there are 9 doughnuts left over. The teacher asks the class to figure out what fraction of the doughnuts remain. You say that say that 1/4 of the doughnuts are left. David says that you are wrong—that 9/36 of them remain. How will you explain to David that your answer was correct?

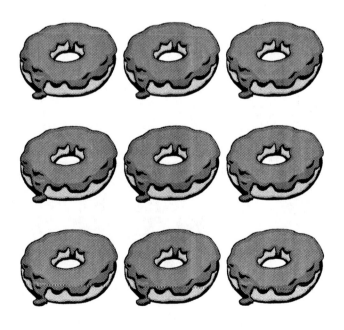

A PIECE OF PIE

26. Suppose your mother baked an apple pie and your sister ate half of it. Then your brother came in and ate half of what she left. The next day your mother ate half of what your brother left. You ate the rest. How will you figure out what fraction of the original pie you ate?

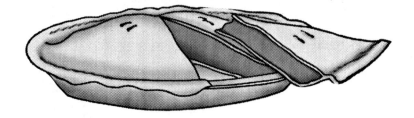

27. Add the next row of ice cream cones to continue the pattern. Explain how you knew what to draw next.

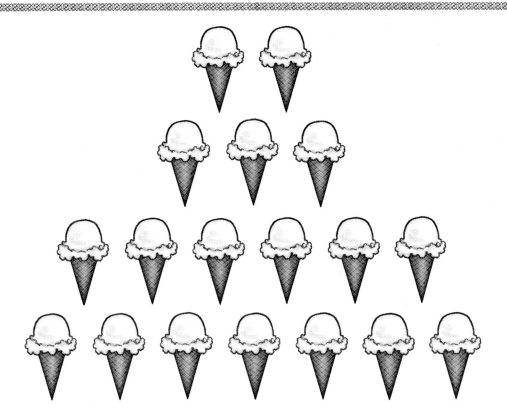

A REWARD

28. Rebecca found a wallet on her way home from school. When she looked inside, she found the phone number of the person who lost it. She called the woman and told her that she had found her wallet. The woman told Rebecca to keep 15% as a reward. Rebecca kept $30. How will you figure out how much money was in the wallet?

© Educational Impressions, Inc.

DIVIDING FRACTIONS

29. Use complete sentences to explain how you would solve the following problem. Be sure to include the term *reciprocal* in your explanation.

$$3/4 \div 1/8 =$$

MULTIPLYING FRACTIONS

30. Use complete sentences to explain how you would solve the following problem. Include the following terms in your explanation: *numerator, denominator, reduce, mixed number,* and *improper fraction.*

$$2\ 1/3 \times 1/4 =$$

31. What is the difference between common multiples and common factors? Use the two sets of numbers below in your explanation.

8	16	24	32	40	48	56	64
6	12	18	24	30	36	42	48

1	2	3	4	6	12
1	2	3	6	9	18

GREAT CIRCLES

32. A great circle is any circle that divides the earth into two equal halves. The shortest distance between two points on the earth or on a globe is called a great circle route. Explain which of the imaginary lines on a globe are great circles.

BIRTHDAY MONEY

33. Sam receives $150 in birthday presents and goes to the mall to spend it. In the department store he spends $21.40 on jeans, $64.20 for sneakers, and $16.05 for a shirt. Then he goes to the sports store and buys a basketball for $22.47. As he is about to leave, he passes a video-game store. The game he wants would cost him $32.10, but he does not know if he has enough money left. Assuming $150 was all he had, how will he determine if he has enough?

THE SHRINKING SNOWGIRL

34. You and your friends built a 10-foot-tall snowgirl on Saturday. On Sunday, however, the weather turned warmer. The snowgirl melted until it was only 90% of its original height. On Monday, it melted some more until it was 3/4 of the height it was on Sunday. How tall was the snowgirl when it stopped melting on Monday? Explain in detail how you arrived at your answer.

USING A PROTRACTOR

35. Write a detailed explanation of how to draw and measure an angle using a protractor.

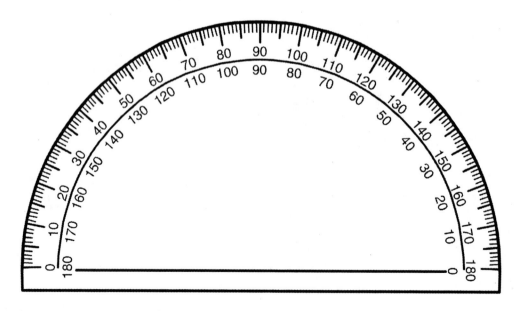

PAIRS OF ANGLES

36. Use the terms *adjacent*, *complementary* and *supplementary* to explain the relationships between the angles in each pair of angles below.

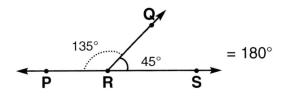

= 180°

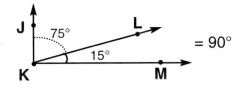

= 90°

WILL WE EVER MEET?

37. What is the word that describes the relationship between these two lines? If points B and P are 3 inches apart, how far apart are points C and M? Explain how you know.

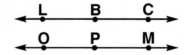

WHERE'S THE FRUIT?

38. The mountain gorilla consumes parts of at least 142 plant species and only 3 types of fruit; that is because there is little fruit available due to the high altitude. How would you express the ratio of fruit types to plant species?

WHAT A WAY TO MEET!

39. Describe the relationship between these two lines. Be sure to include the following terms: *degree, perpendicular, right angle,* and *intersect.*

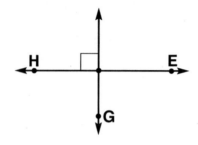

BATTING AVERAGE

40. When Jake asked what was meant by "batting average," the coach explained that it was the percentage of times the batter gets a successful hit. Jake knew that he had 20 at bats and that he got 6 successful hits. How will he figure out his batting average? Use ratio terms to describe what this means.

PANCAKE-EATING CONTEST

41. Your town held a pancake-eating contest. There were 30 finalists. In the final round a total of 275 pancakes were eaten. The winner ate 25 of them. What was the average number of pancakes eaten by the finalists? What percentage of the pancakes were eaten by the winner? Explain in complete sentences how you would figure out the answers to these questions.

DESCRIBE THAT POLYGON

42. Name and describe the figure to the right in as much detail as possible. Include the following terms: *sides, vertices,* and *internal angles.*

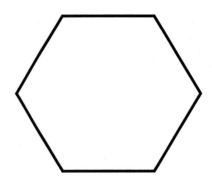

WHY NOT?

43. You have been asked to explain to a younger child why all parallelograms are quadrilaterals but not all quadrilaterals are parallelograms. What will you say?

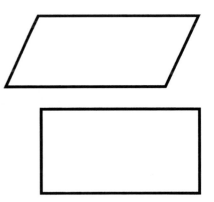

A PICKY PANCAKE EATER

44. Mike was extremely fussy. When his mother made him pancakes for breakfast, he insisted that each pancake be a circle with a diameter of exactly 4 inches. What was the circumference of each pancake? What was the surface area of each pancake? Explain in complete sentences how you arrive at each answer.

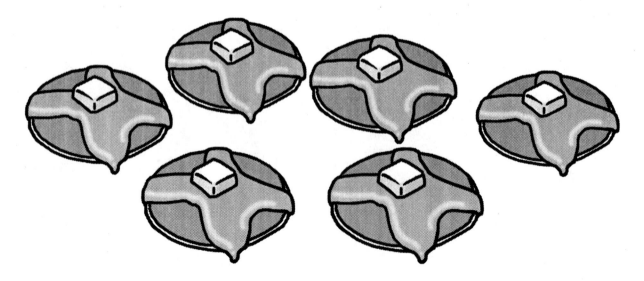

WHICH FRAME?

45. Penny went to a shop called Just Frames. She told the clerk that she wanted a square frame with a perimeter of 1 1/3 feet. The clerk had 2 square frames. One of them measured 4 inches on each side. The other measured 3 inches on each side. How will the clerk determine which one to show Penny?

SHARE AND SHARE ALIKE

46. You and your friend Emma are sharing a personal pizza. You have the pie cut into four equal pieces. What is the measure of each interior angle?

Nicholas and Sam are also sharing a personal pizza; however, they ask that their pie be cut in half. What angle is formed?

Emily, Josh, and Jake are sharing a personal pizza too; however, theirs is cut into eight equal pieces. What type of interior angles result?

Explain how you arrived at each answer.

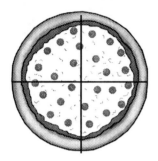 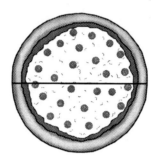 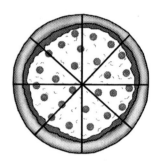

SO MANY ELEPHANTS!

47. The owner of the Big Time Circus wants to create a spectacular act using a Pattern of Elephants. He already has 33 elephants—enough for the first six rows of the pattern he has in mind. He tells tells his assistant to find enough elephants for one more row. How many more elephants will the assistant have to find? Explain in complete sentences how you arrived at your answer.

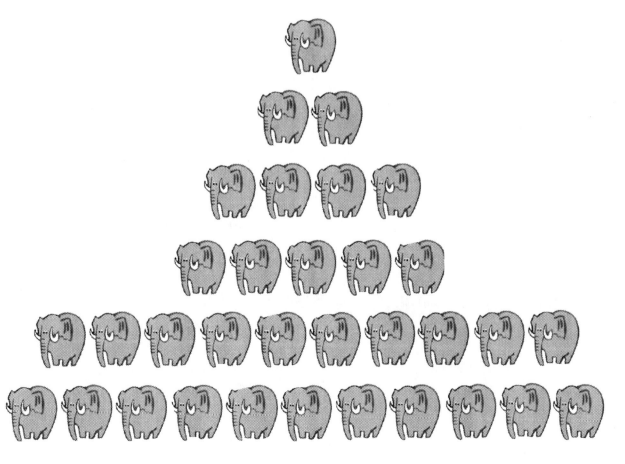

A DIVISION PROBLEM

48. In complete sentences explain all the steps you would have to take in order to solve this problem. Include the following terms in your explanation: *dividend, divisor, quotient* and *remainder.*

$735 \div 16 =$

ORDER OF OPERATIONS

49. Your teacher puts this problem on the board: 3 x 8 – 16 ÷ 4 + 1 =. She asks who can solve it. Your friend says that the answer is 3. You say it is 21. Your teacher asks you to explain why 21 is the correct answer. What will you say?

$$3 \times 8 - 16 \div 4 + 1 \neq 3$$

$$3 \times 8 - 16 \div 4 + 1 = 21$$

50. Put these in order from least to greatest and explain in detail how you arrived at your answer.

$$.791 \qquad 4/5 \qquad 79\%$$

MAKING CHANGE

51. You get a summer job working at a pet shop. A customer's bill comes to $25.68. He gives you a $50 bill. You give him $24.32 change. He says that you owe him an additional $10. Explain to him in detail how you arrived at the $24.32.

PIZZA PARTY

52. You and your friends ordered two pizza pies. The shaded area represents the slices you and your friends ate. Matt thinks that 3/4 of the total amount of pizza was eaten, but you know that he is wrong. Write an explanation to help him understand how much pizza was eaten. How many more slices would have to be eaten for him to be correct?

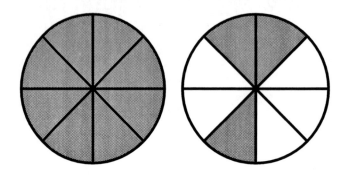

THAT'S IMPOSSIBLE

53. Your friend thinks that 2 x 1/2 is 2.5. Without solving the problem, explain to her why this is impossible.

2 x 1/2 = ?

A FACTOR TREE

54. Prime factorization can be accomplished by creating a factor tree. Using complete sentences, explain what is meant by prime factorization and write directions on how to create a factor tree.

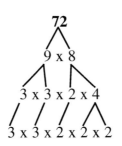

LESS THAN, GREATER THAN OR EQUAL?

55. Use the symbols =, <, and > in sentences that compare these numbers. Be sure to include each number and each symbol in at least one sentence.

1/5   .20   2   1.1   60%

A BLOCK PARTY

56. Your neighborhood is having a block party. There will be hot dogs, hamburgers, french fries and ice cream. You are in charge of ordering the hot dogs. How will you figure out how many hot dogs to order? First write down all the information you will need. Then explain the steps you will take to use that information.to figure out the number of hot dogs you must order.

A MATH TEST

57. Your teacher writes the following results of the math test on the board. She asks you to figure out the class average, the median score, the range, and the mode. How will you do it?

2 students: 100%
3 students: 90%
8 students: 85%
7 students: 80%
2 students: 70%

CIRCLE CONFUSION

58. The diameter of this circle is 3 inches. Your friend says that the area of the circle is about 9.42 square inches. Explain to him why he is wrong. Use the terms *circumference, diameter, radius,* and *pi* in your explanation.

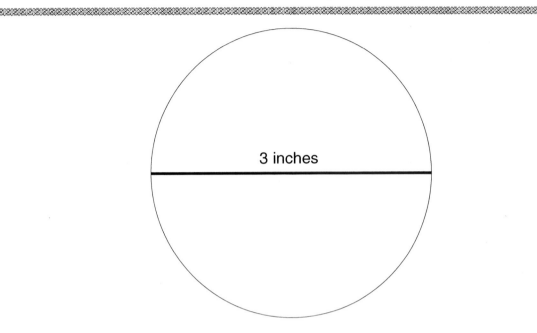

3 inches

FENCED IN

59. Your family just rescued a dog from the pound. Your mother asks you to figure out how much fencing you will need. She also wants to know how many square yards will be enclosed. The area to be fenced in is a rectangle with the following dimensions: 40 feet, 40 feet, 20 feet and 20 feet. How will you figure out how much fencing will be needed? How will you figure out how many square yards will be within the fence?

ICE-CREAM PARTY

60. Your family is having a large ice-cream party. Your mom figures that there should be 15 quarts of ice cream and asks you to go to the store to buy them. When you get to the store, there are only gallons. How will you figure out how many gallon containers to buy?

AT THE ZOO

61. You are at the zoo and are standing outside watching the chimpanzees play. You count four chimpanzees. The zookeeper tells you that 75% of the chimps are inside. You want to know the total number of chimps. Explain how you will figure it out.

HALLOWEEN CANDY

62. You bought 7 pounds of candy to give out on Halloween. If each child is to be given 1/8 pound, how many portions of candy do you have? Explain how you know.

DIGIT DETAILS

63. Read the number below. In complete sentences explain what each digit in the number means.

4,392,786

HOW MANY TABLESPOONS?

64. You are following a recipe that calls for 1/4 cup of milk. You cannot find your cup measure. In fact, the only measure you can find is a tablespoon. Your sister says you should add 8 tablespoons. Explain to her why she is wrong.

THE BIGGEST BALLOON

65. You take your younger cousin to the park and she begs you for a balloon. She wants you to buy her the largest one. The salesman tells you that the red balloon measures 3.5 feet in circumference, the blue balloon measures 38 inches in diameter, and the green balloon measures 3 1/4 feet in diameter. Which one will you choose so that your cousin has the largest? Explain how you made your decision.

GIGANTIC GIRAFFES

66. Your favorite animal at the zoo is the giraffe. The zookeeper tells you that the adult male giraffe is about 18 feet in height and that the adult female giraffe is about 14 feet in height. What fraction of the male's height is the female's height. Express the fraction in its simplest terms. Explain how you arrived at your answer.

HOW MANY MILES?

67. A truck driver drove 57 1/4 miles from Newark, DE, to Baltimore, MD. Then he drove 38 1/8 miles to Washington, DC. Finally, he drove 264 3/4 miles to Raleigh, NC. Explain how you will figure out how many miles he drove in total.

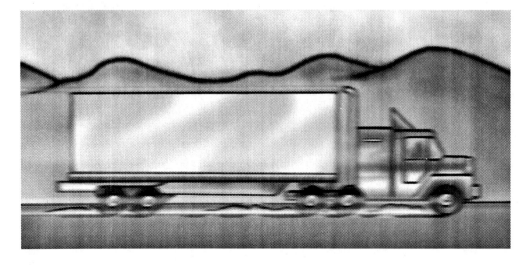

HOW MANY SERVINGS?

68. There are 20 cakes. If each serving is 1/4 cake, how many servings are there? Explain how you will find out.

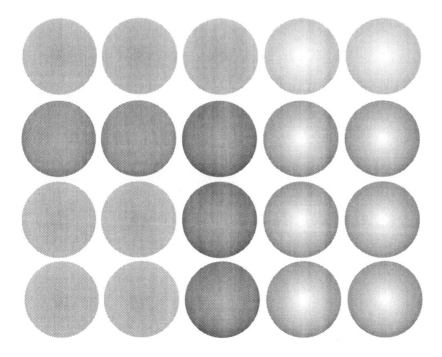

GENRE CHOICES

69. The following graph shows the number of students in Oakwood Public School who chose each genre for their reading assignment. What percentage of the students chose either an adventure or a mystery book? Tell in complete sentences how you arrived at your answer.

OAKWOOD PUBLIC SCHOOL

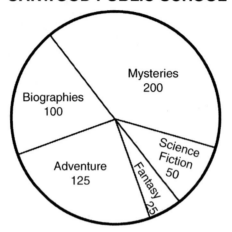

© Educational Impressions, Inc.

A PILE OF JUNK

70. Your dad has asked you to use the wheelbarrow to clear out a huge pile of junk. In the first trip you carry away 1/4 of the pile. In the second trip you carry away 1/3 of the original pile. In the third trip you carry away 1/6 of the original pile. At that point your dad asks you what fraction of the original pile is left? Explain in complete sentences how you will figure out what to tell him.

PANDA FEAST

71. You have been watching the panda eat bamboo for an hour. In the first 15 minutes it ate 9 1/2 stalks. In the next 15 minutes it ate 10 3/4 stalks. In the next 15 minutes it ate 12 5/8 stalks. In the last 15 minutes it ate 11 3/8 stalks. How many stalks did the panda eat in the hour? Explain in detail how you arrived at the answer.

DOUBLE BAR GRAPH

72. This graph shows the number of books read by fourth graders in Valley Elementary School and Eastville Elementary School. In which year did the students of Valley School read more books than the students of Eastville? Write an explanation that would help a younger child who is unfamiliar with bar graphs figure out the answer.

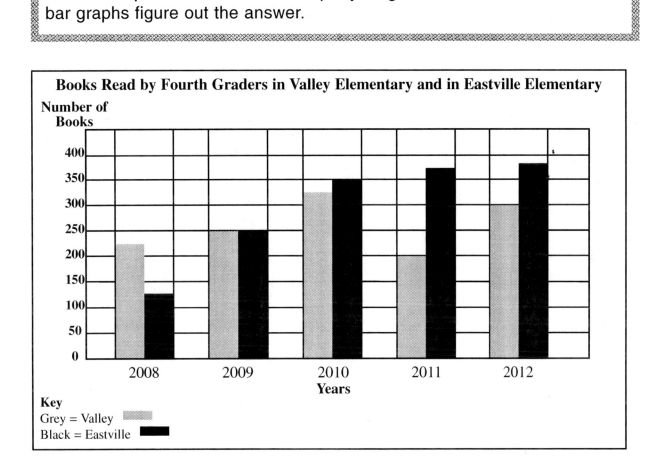

CUBIC INCHES

73. Your friend thinks the volume of this cube is 25 cubic inches. Write what you will say to him to make him realize he is wrong?

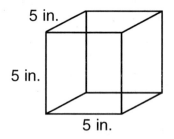

5 in.

5 in.

5 in.

BIRTHDAY COOKIES

74. Sara brought 72 cookies to class for her birthday. Her teacher said that if she could tell her what percentage of the cookies had been eaten, she could take the leftovers home. Nine cookies were left. How will Sara figure out what percentage was eaten?

© Educational Impressions, Inc.

PROTECT THE SAPLING

75. Your class has planted a small sapling in the exact center of a small circular area. The tree is exactly 10 feet from the edge of the field. Your teacher wants to put a fence around the circular field to protect the sapling. Explain how you will figure out how much fencing is needed.

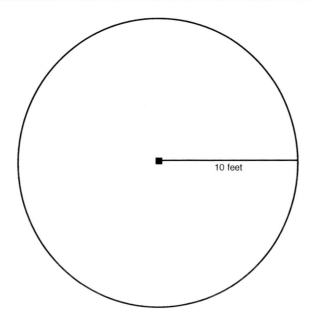

10 feet

PRIME OR COMPOSITE?

76. Explain what is meant by a prime number and a composite number. Why are some numbers are called relatively prime numbers? Give examples of each.

Prime Numbers?

Composite Numbers?

77. Below is a double line graph comparing the number of foul shots made by Nick and Beth. What other kind of graph could have been used? Do you think the double line graph was the best choice? Give reasons for your opinion.

Beth's and Nick's Foul Shots

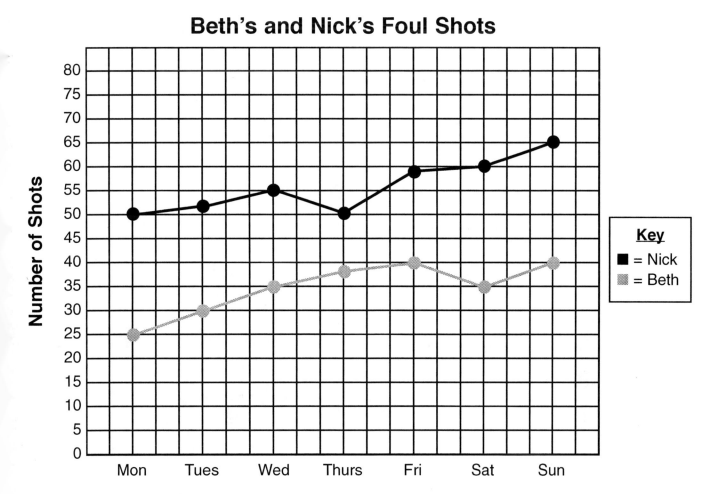

A FISH STORY

78. Your brother went fishing with his friends. When he returned home, he told about a huge fish that he had caught and had thrown back into the water. He said that the fish was 22 inches in length. Later you heard him tell his friend that the fish was 2 1/4 feet long. When your parents came home from shopping, he told them that the fish was 55 inches in length. How much did the fish grow with each story? Explain how you figured this out.

PIÑATA PARTY

79. There are 149 pieces of candy in the piñata. Elena does not think there will be enough candy for each of the 36 children to get 4 pieces when the piñata breaks. Her older sister Maria tells her not to worry. She says there is more than enough. What might Maria say to Elena so that she will understand why there is enough?

THE 100th DAY OF SCHOOL

80. For the 100th day of school each child in the kindergarten class was asked to bring in 100 of something. Zack brought in 100 marbles. Forty percent of his marbles were green; 21 percent were yellow; 18 percent were tan; and the rest were grey. How many were grey? Explain how you will figure this out.

81. In complete sentences write everything you can learn from this graph.

Key

Cherry Swirl = (CS)
Cotton Candy = (CC)
Pink Mix Sundae = (PM)
Yummy Delight = (YD)
Fluffy Pink Surprise (FP)

"Name That Ice Cream" Voting Results

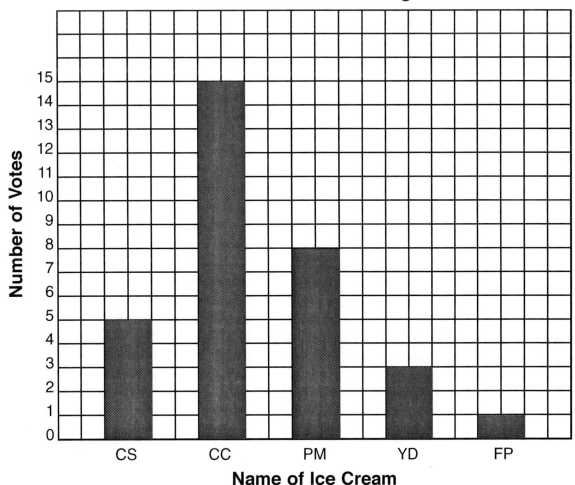

Number of Votes

Name of Ice Cream

WHAT'S ITS VALUE?

82. In complete sentences compare each 7 in 777 to the other two digits in the number.

777

WHAT'S THE RATIO?

83. You want to know the ratio of dark sheep to light sheep. Explain how you will figure it out.

PRACTICE MAKES PERFECT

84. Zack practiced his guitar after school every day this week. On Monday through Wednesday he practiced from 4:00 p.m. to 5:15 p.m. On Thursday and Friday he practiced from 4:00 p.m. to 4:50 p.m. He also practiced on Saturday from 10:20 a.m. until 11:50 a.m. and on Sunday from 11:35 a.m. until 1:46 p.m. On Sunday night, his mother asked him how many hours he had practiced this week. Explain how he will figure out how the number of hours.

ADDING FRACTIONS

85. Write directions for adding fractions with like denominators. Use the terms *numerator* and *denominator* in your explanation. Explain what to do if your answer is an improper fraction.

$$\frac{3}{5} \ + \ \frac{4}{5} \ =$$

SUBTRACTING FRACTIONS

86. Write directions for subtracting fractions with like denominators. Use the terms *numerator* and *denominator* in your explanation.

$$\frac{6}{7} \ - \ \frac{4}{7} \ =$$

A YARD OF RIBBON

87. You need a total of 1 yard of ribbon. You have two pieces. One measures 15 1/4 inches and the other measures 22 3/8 inches. How will you determine if you have enough ribbon?

15 $\frac{1}{4}$ inches
22 $\frac{3}{8}$ inches

PAYING THE BILL

88. You and two friends go out to lunch. You order 2 hamburgers at $5.00 each, 1 cheeseburger at $6.00, and 3 ice-cream sodas at $2.50 each. There is no tax, but you want to leave a 20% tip. If you want to share the bill equally, how will you figure out how much each of you has to pay?

MULTIPLYING FRACTIONS

89. Explain each step you would take to solve this multiplication problem. Use the terms *numerator*, *denominator* and *product* in your explanation.

$$\frac{3}{5} \; \text{x} \; \frac{4}{5} \; =$$

DIVIDING FRACTIONS

90. Explain each step you would take to solve this division problem. Use the terms *numerator*, *denominator* and *quotient* in your explanation.

$$\frac{3}{5} \; \div \; \frac{4}{5} \; =$$

A RECTANGULAR PRISM

91. Explain why this chest is a rectangular prism. Suppose its dimensions were 25 inches by 22 inches by 16 inches. Write an equation that shows how you would find its volume.

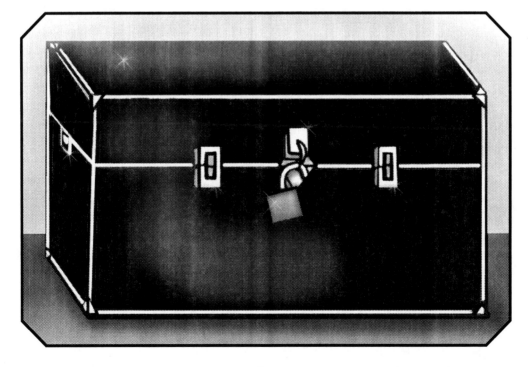

HOW MANY EGGS?

92. Your mother needs 5 1/2 dozen eggs and asks you to go to the store to buy them. When you get there, the clerk tells you that the only eggs left are in cartons of 36. How will you figure out how many cartons to buy?

A NEW RECORD

93. Emma has the new record for her school's foul-shooting contest. Every contestant had 100 shots. Emma made 20% more baskets than the school's previous record holder. The previous record holder made 70 baskets out of one hundred tries. How will you figure out how many baskets Emma made?

AN AVID READER

94. Melissa loves to read. She has a list of 20 books that she wants to take out of the library. The librarian tells her that 15% of them are not available. Melissa wants to know how many books she WILL be able to take home. Explain how she will figure it out.

95. Explain what B and C represent in each diagram. Use the terms *ray, line segment, line, and point* in your explanation.

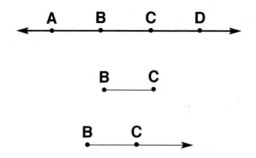

A PORTION OF PEANUTS

96. You and 3 friends go to a baseball game and buy 3 large bags of peanuts. The 4 of you want to share equally. Explain how you will figure out the size of each person's share.

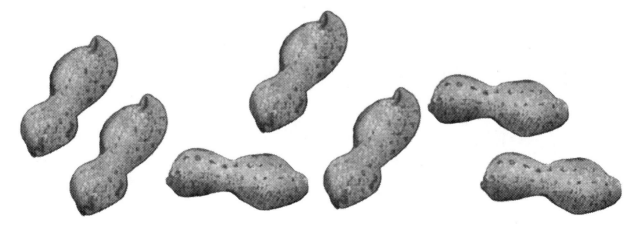

A SPORTS ARTICLE

97. Your local high school has just held a contest to see who can kick the longest field goal. You are writing an article for the school newspaper and would like to include the range, mean, mode and median of the finalists' scores. Explain how you will determine each.

These were the scores of the 10 finalists:

29 yards
58 yards
40 yards
25 yards
48 yards
36 yards
29 yards
47 yards
29 yards
41 yards

A BIGGER GARDEN

98. Your garden is 6 feet by 2 feet. You want to enlarge it so that it has an area of 24 square feet. There is no room to make the 6-foot side any larger. How much larger will you have to make the 2-foot side in order to get the area you desire? Explain how you arrived at your answer.

IS THERE ENOUGH FOR US?

99. Your mother baked a cake for you and five friends. Four of you each ate 1/8 of the cake. Two of you each ate 1/16 of the cake. Your mother wants to know if there is enough cake left for your father, your brother and her each to have 1/8 of the original cake. How will you figure it out?

WAS THAT MY HOUSE?

100. Isabella walked 11 3/4 blocks from her house to the grocery store. It was raining when she left the store, so she ran home. After running 13 1/6 blocks, she realized that she had passed her house. How many blocks past her house was she? Explain how you arrived at your answer.

MATH TERMS

101. Brainstorm! Write as many words that relate to math as you can. When you are done, categorize your terms.

EVERYDAY MATH

102. Brainstorm and list the ways in which you and members of your family use math in your daily lives (not counting math classes).

IT'S ABOUT TIME

103. How would you explain time to a younger child? Use complete sentences in your explanation and include the terms *seconds, minutes, hours, days, weeks, months* and *years.*

© Educational Impressions, Inc.

104. Think of as many games as you can that require the use of math skills. Choose one game and explain which skills are needed.

A GEOMETRY POEM

105. Write a poem about geometry.

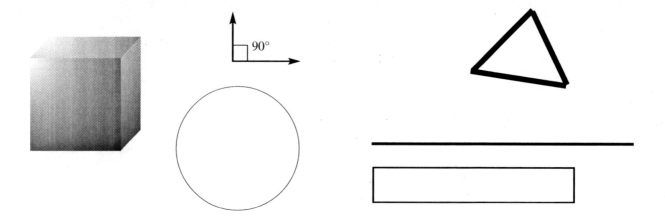

MY HOUSE

106. Describe your house. Use as many math terms as possible.

WHY BOTHER?

107. Discuss why it is important to learn math facts even though you can use a calculator.

YOU'D BE SURPRISED!

108. Write what you might say to someone who thinks math will not be useful in his or her adult life.

THE PERFECT MATH TEACHER

109. You are the superintendent of schools and must hire a new math teacher. What qualifications will you look for when you interview the candidates and read their resumes? Write a recommendation for a candidate in which you explain in detail why you think he or she is well suited for the job.

A SURVEY

110. Survey your classmates to discover their favorite book, TV show, sport, or other topic of your choice. Use a tally to keep track of their responses. Write a summary of your findings.

Holes: ~~||||~~

Maniac Magee: /

Dear Mr. Henshaw: //

ZERO

111. Evaluate the importance of zero. For example, how would you express the number one thousand and ten without it? What would come between +1 and -1?

112. March 14 is Pi Day. Explain why that date was chosen. Design a t-shirt or a bumper sticker using the symbol π in the saying.

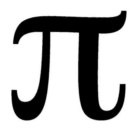

AN ACROSTIC

113. Write an acrostic about mathematics.

M

A

T

H

E

M

A

T

I

C

C

S

STUDY TIPS

114. Explain how you study for a math test.

MATH MAKES ME _____

115. Describe how you feel when math class begins and when it ends.

MATH SYMBOLS

116. Brainstorm to think of as many math symbols as possible. Tell how each is used.

MEASURING TERMS

117. List as many measuring terms as you can. Categorize them.

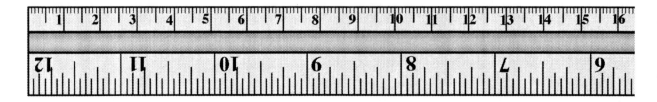

A PERFECT CIRCLE

118. Write directions on how to draw a circle using a compass.

MATH TOOLS

119. List all the tools you can think of that might be necessary to figure out math problems. In complete sentences tell the main use for each.

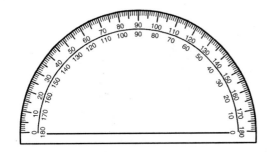

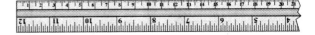

120. Explain the differences among one-dimensional, two-dimensional, and three-dimensional shapes. Provide examples and illustrate your answer.

 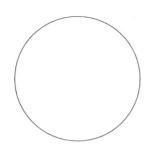 _____

NOTES